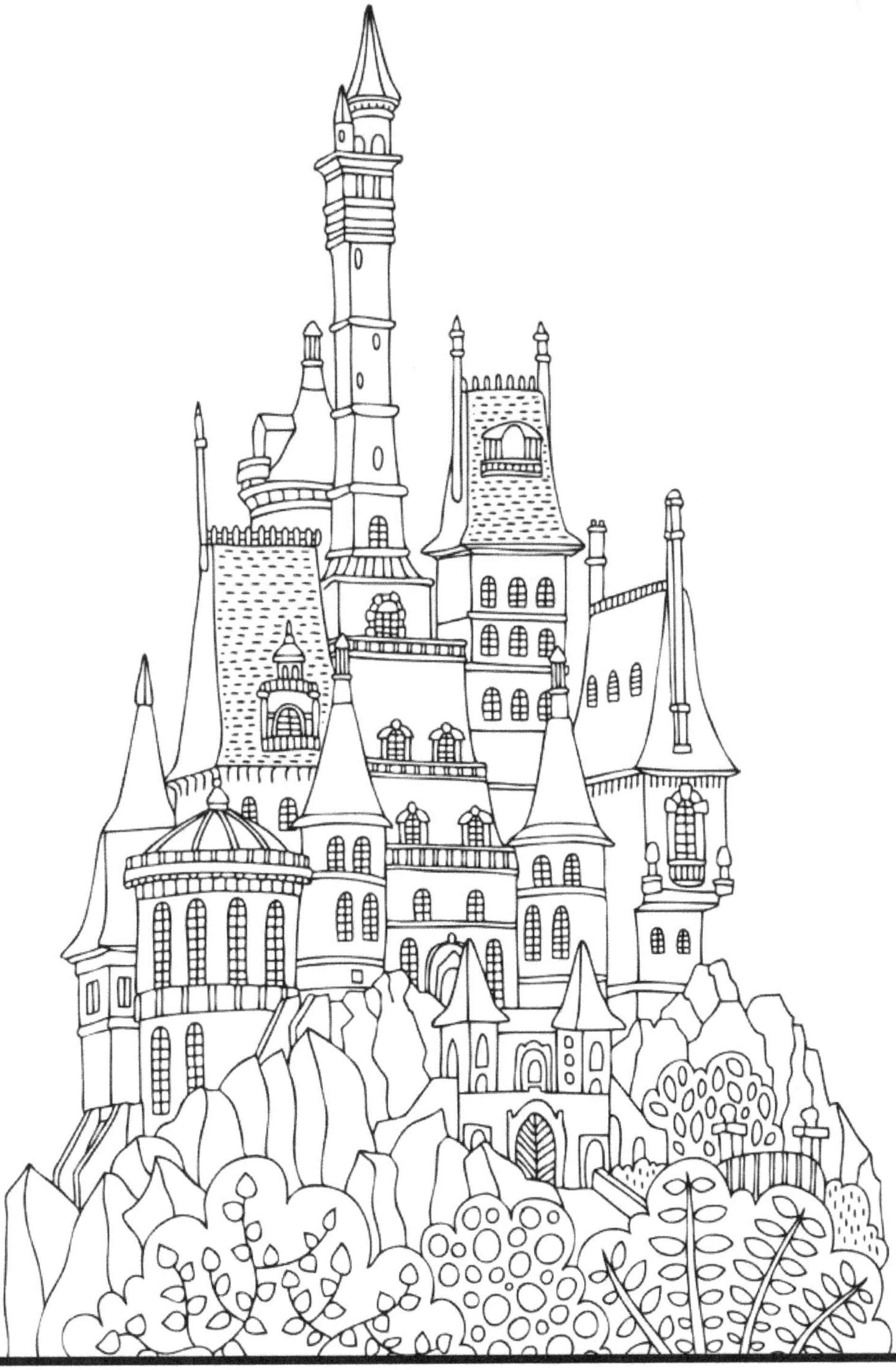

# CASTLES COLORING BOOK

Copyright © 2020 Katrin Stark

ALL RIGHTS RESERVED

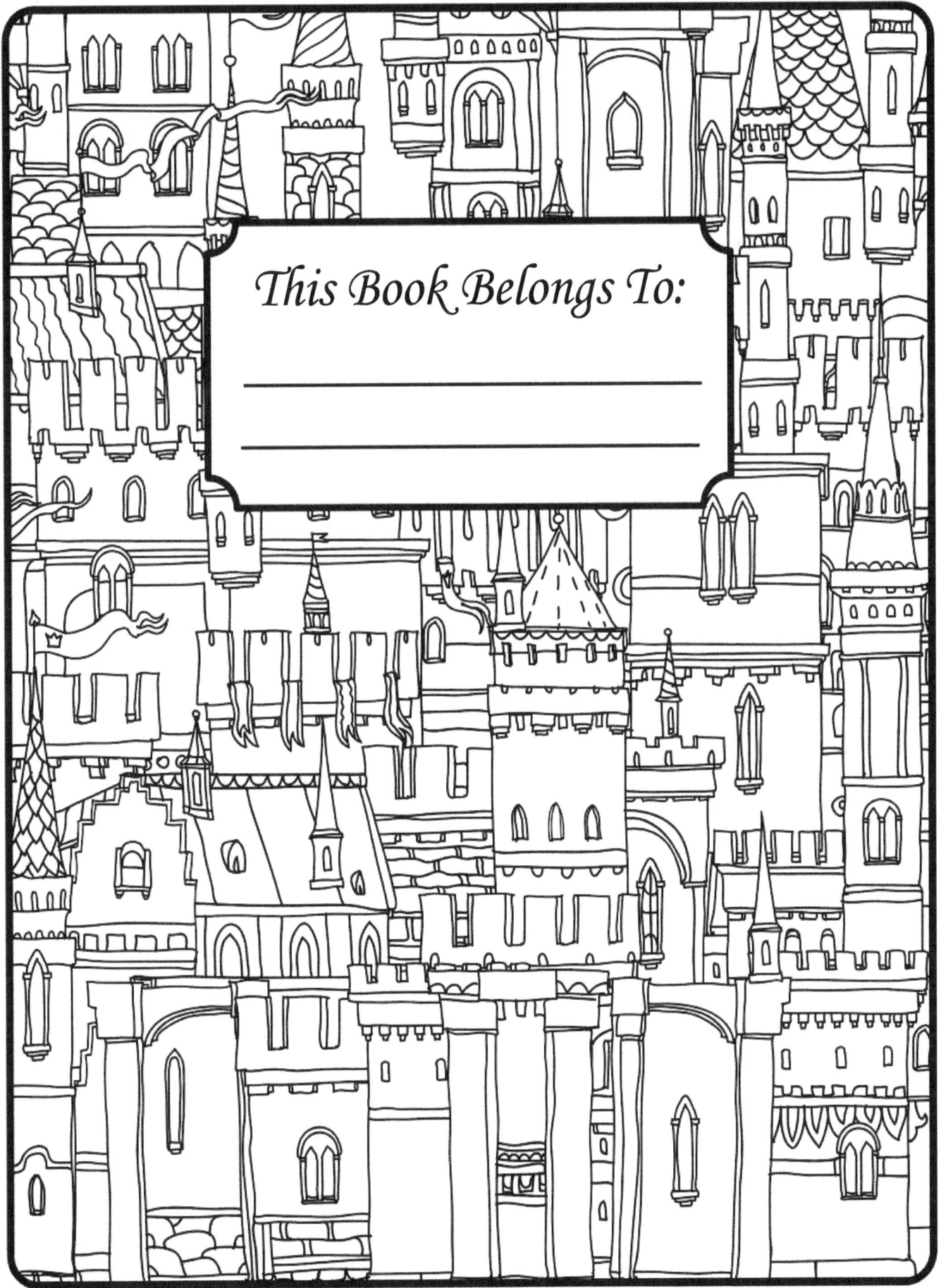

This Book Belongs To:

_____

_____

# COLOR TEST PAGE

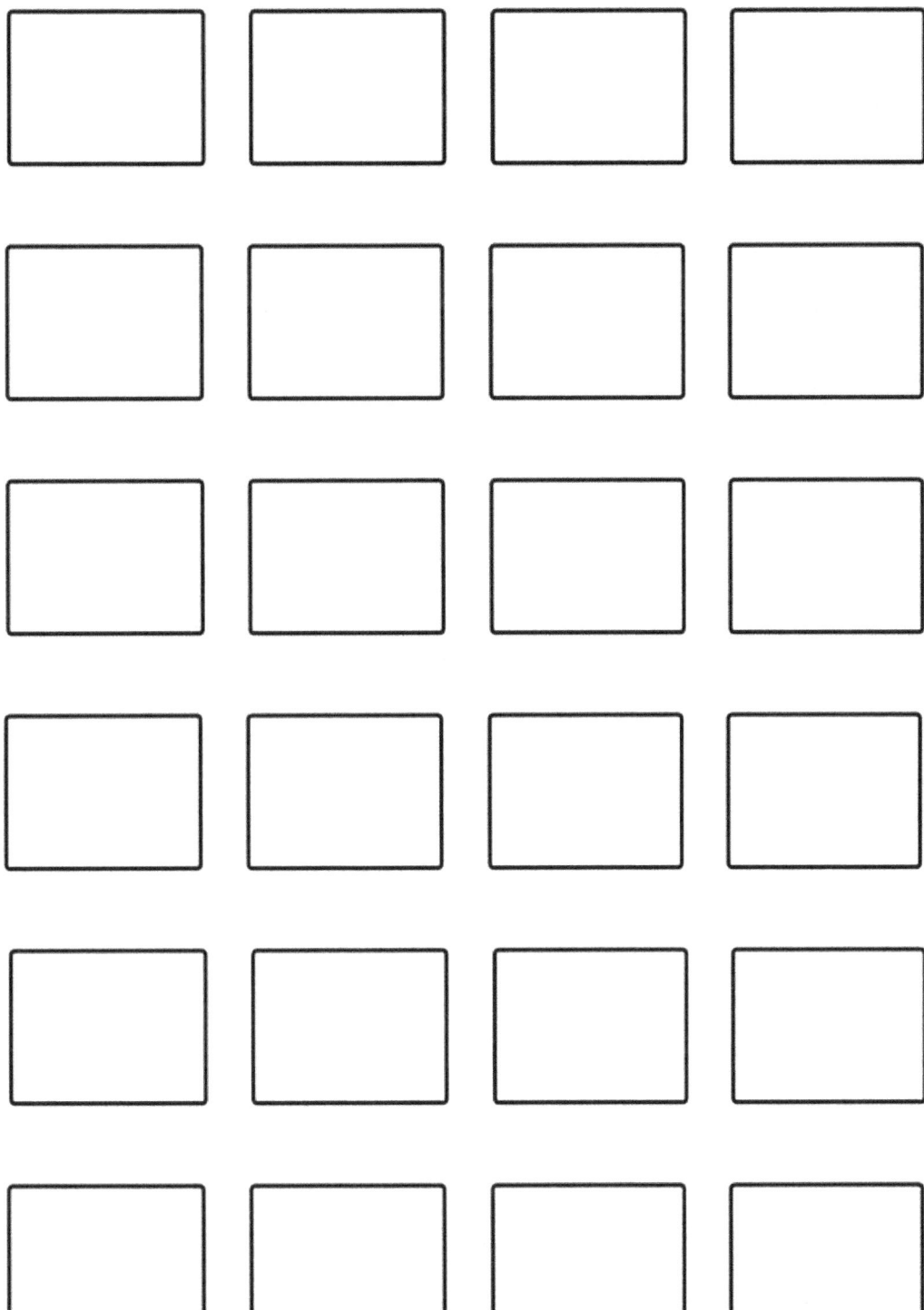

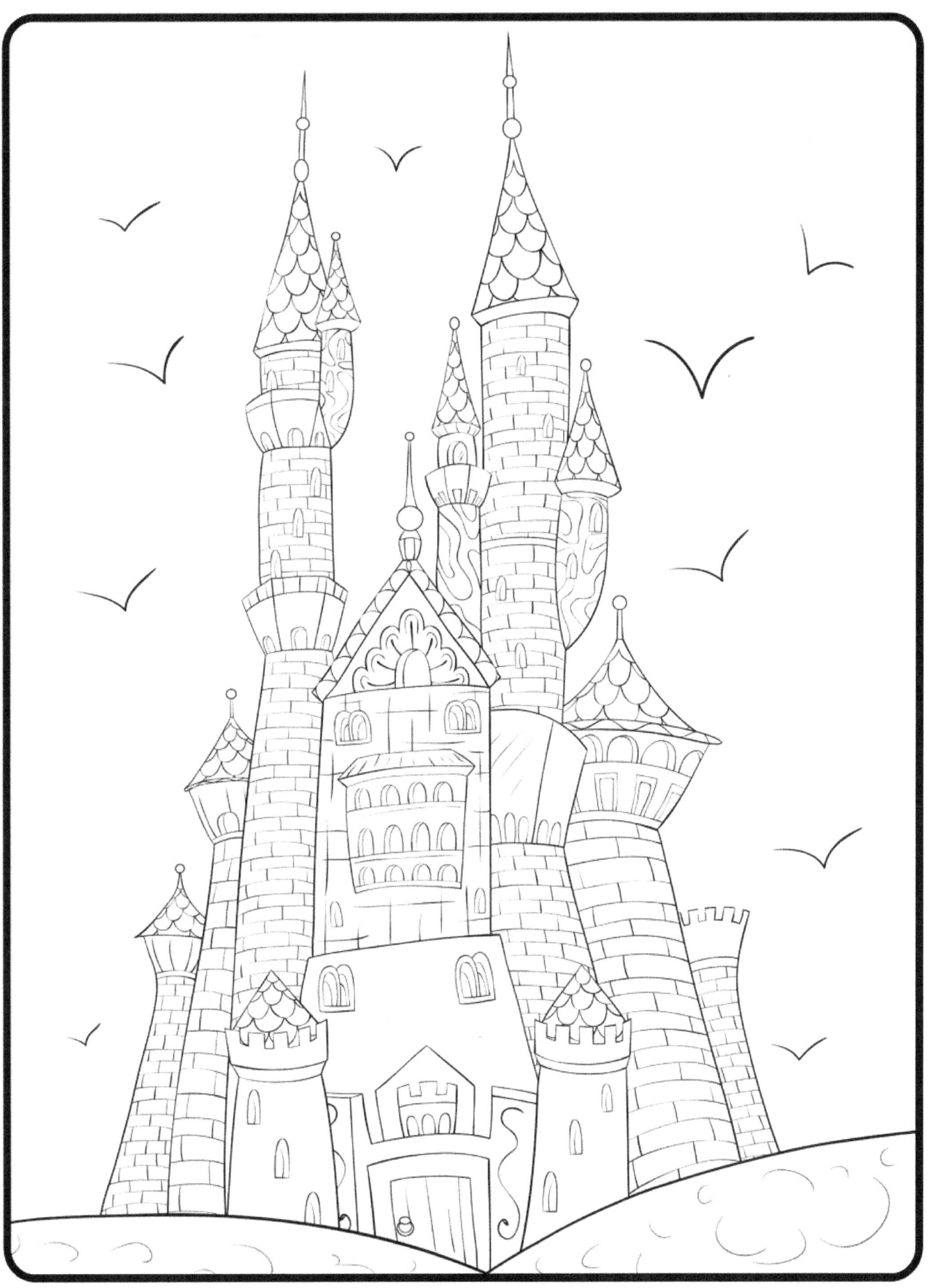

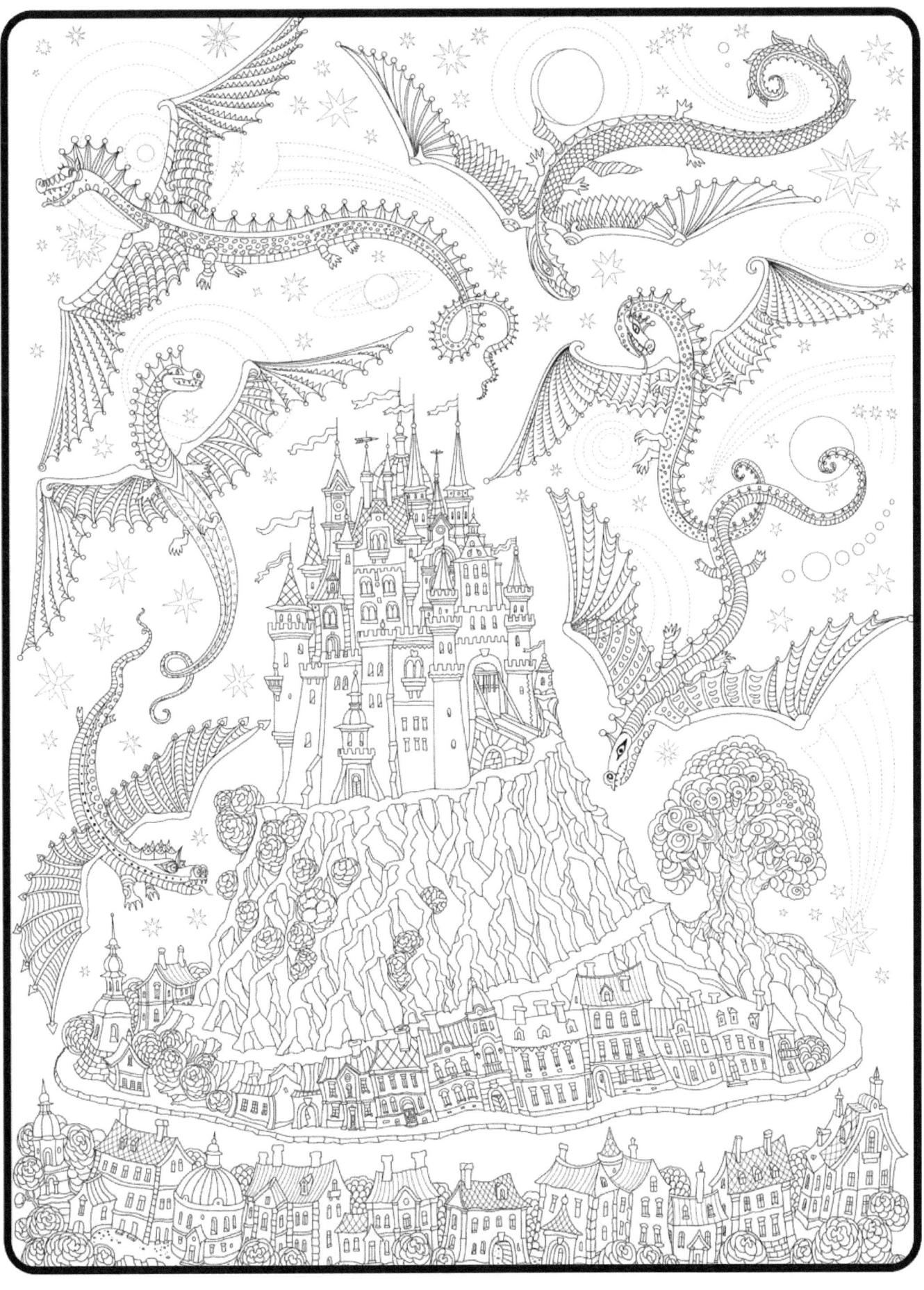

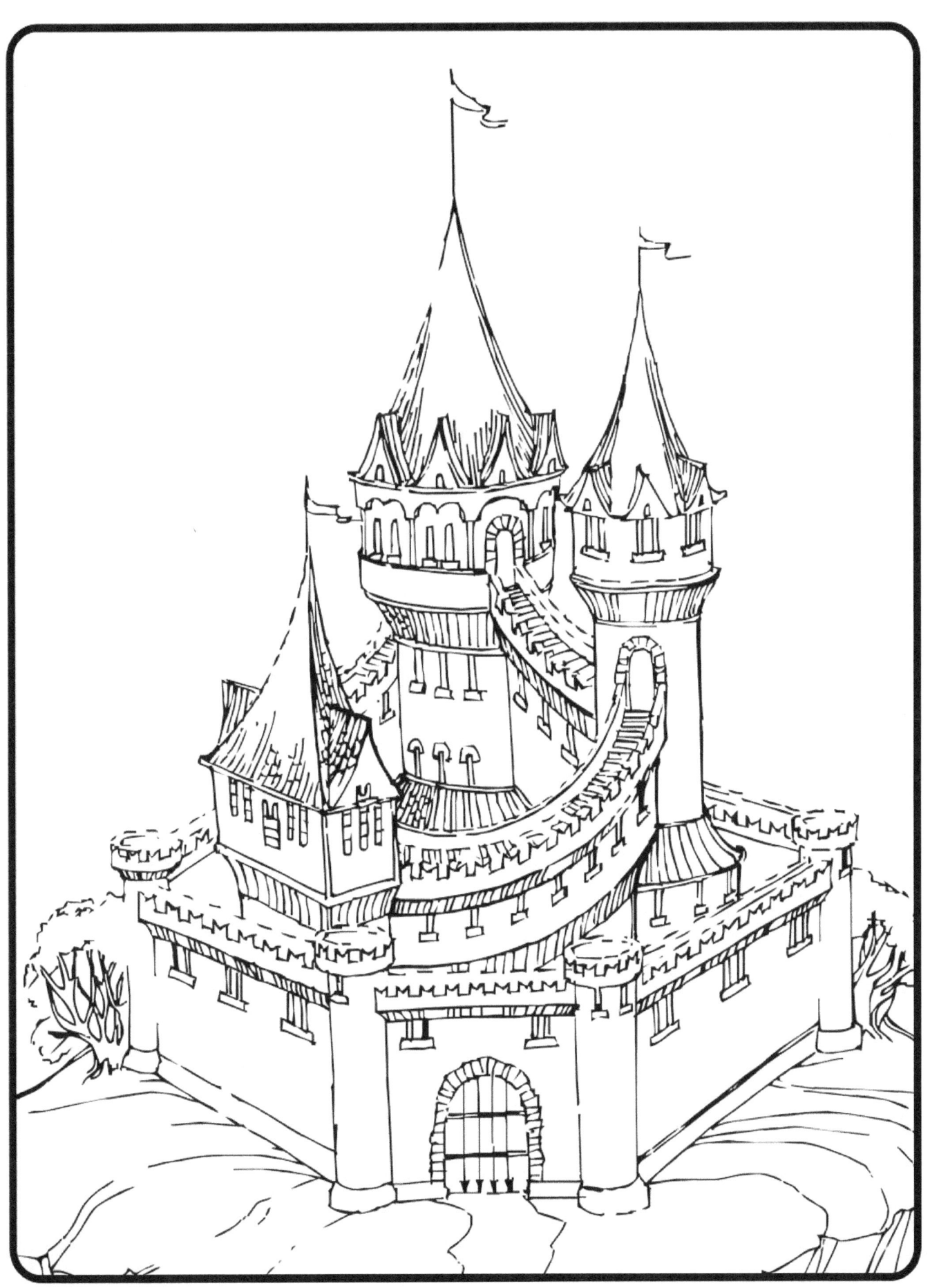

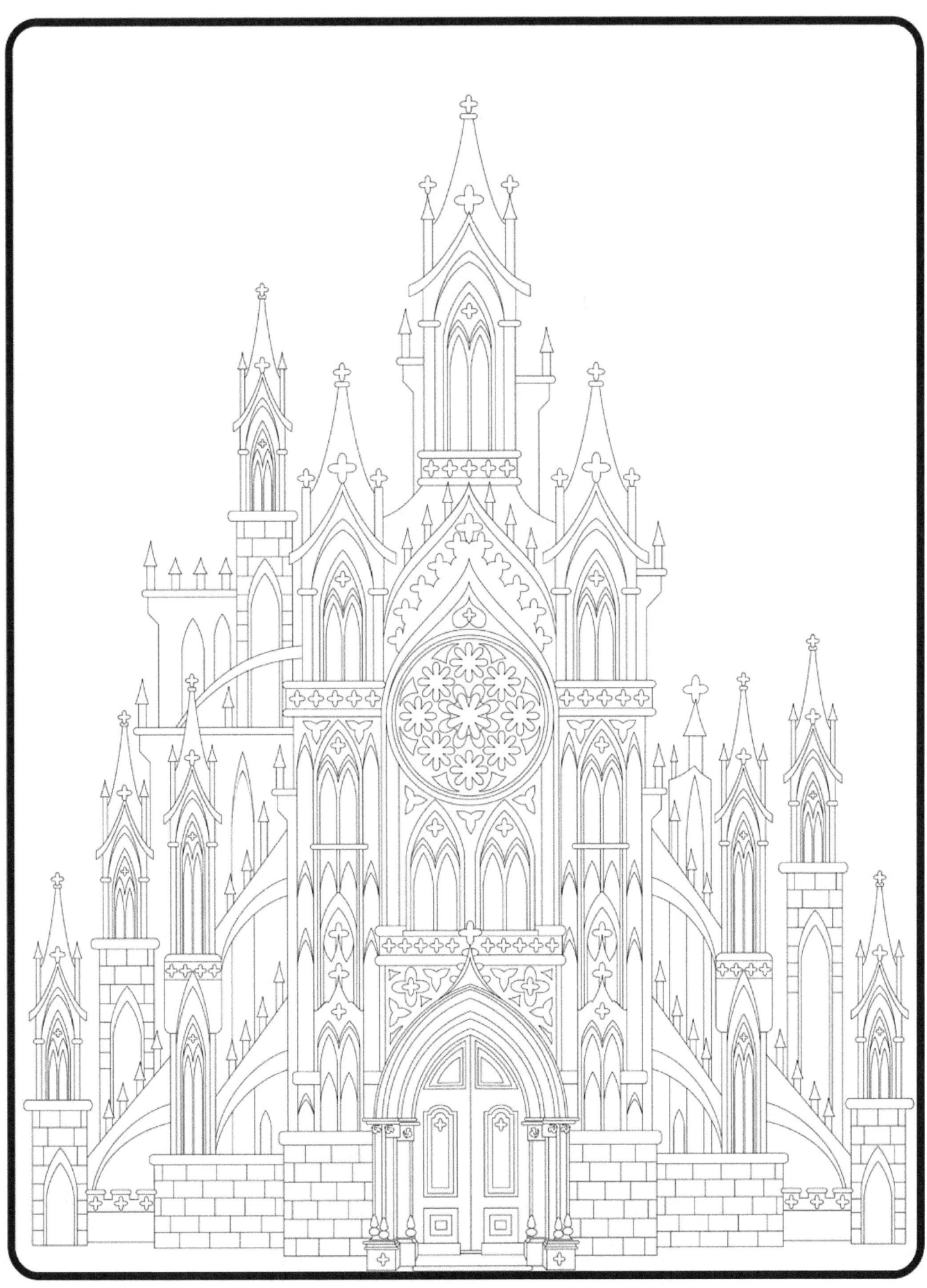

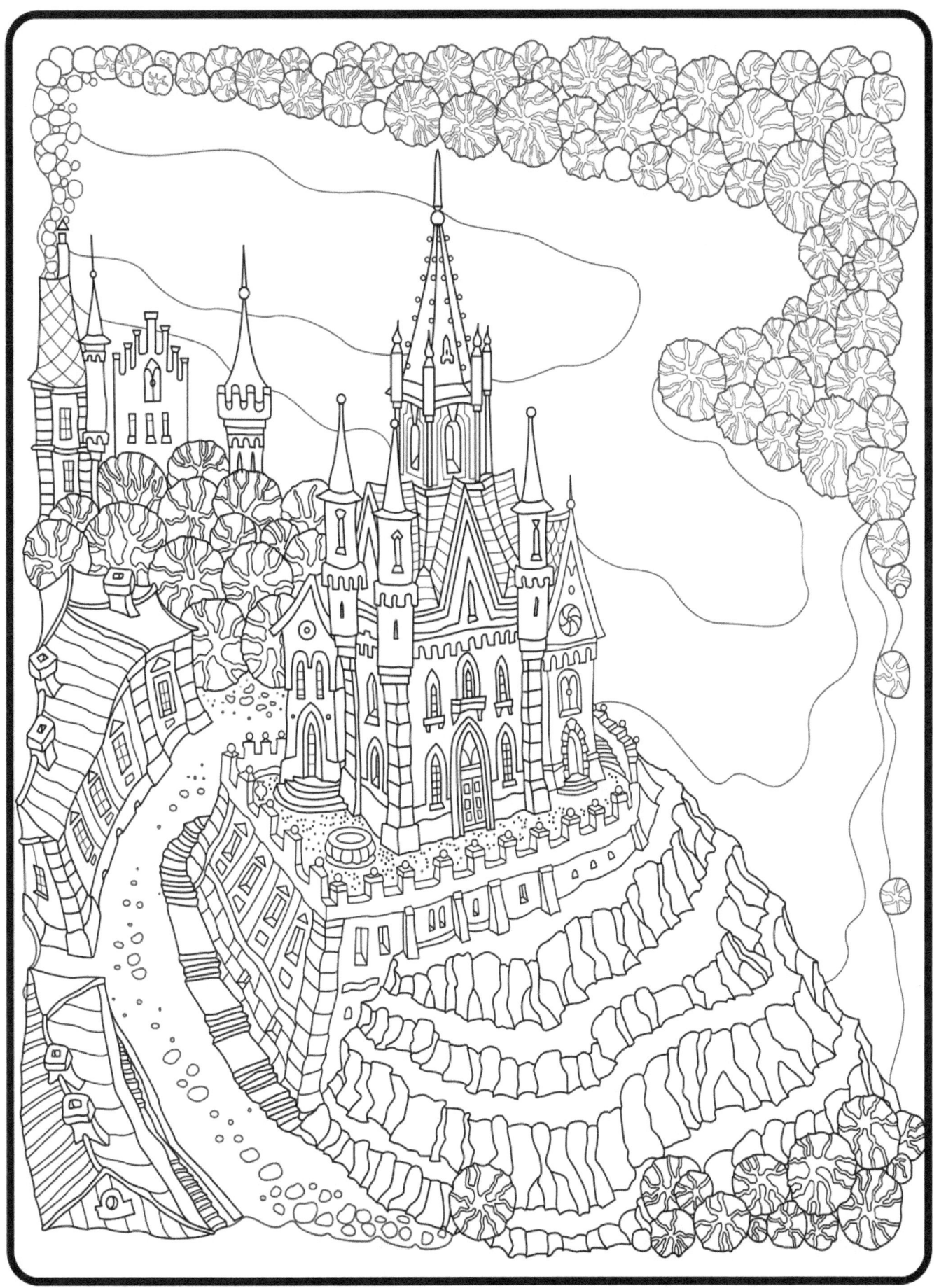

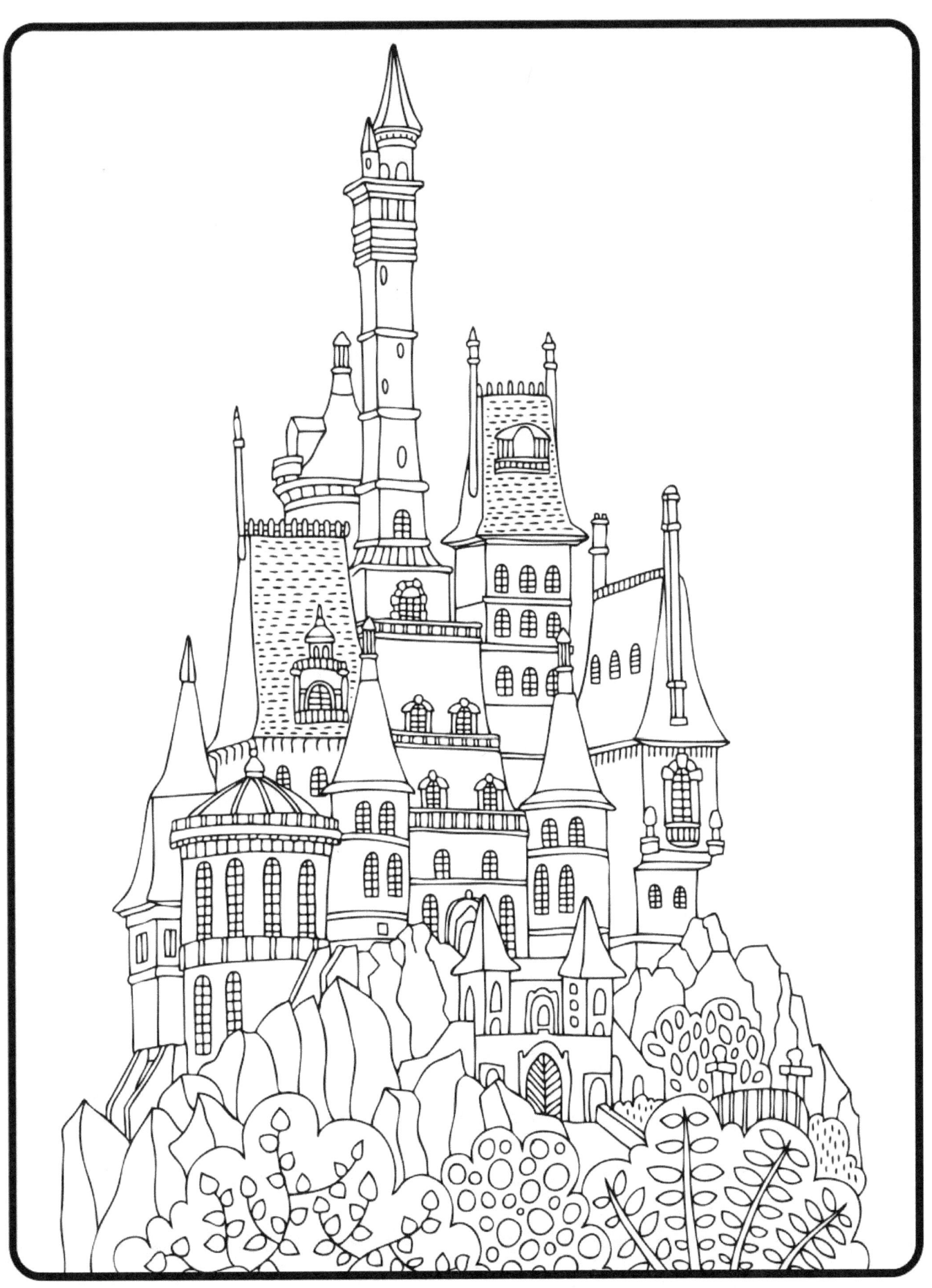

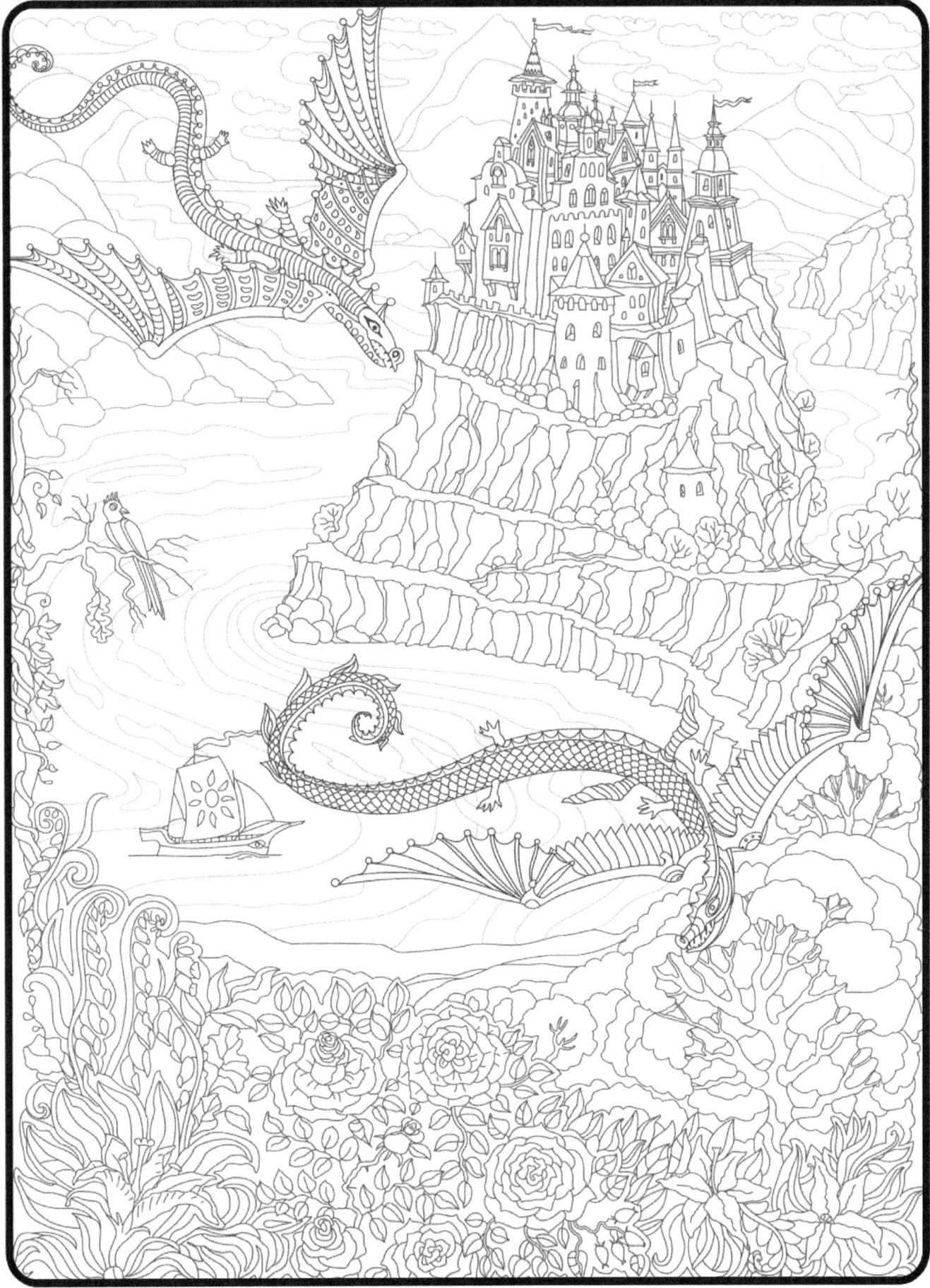

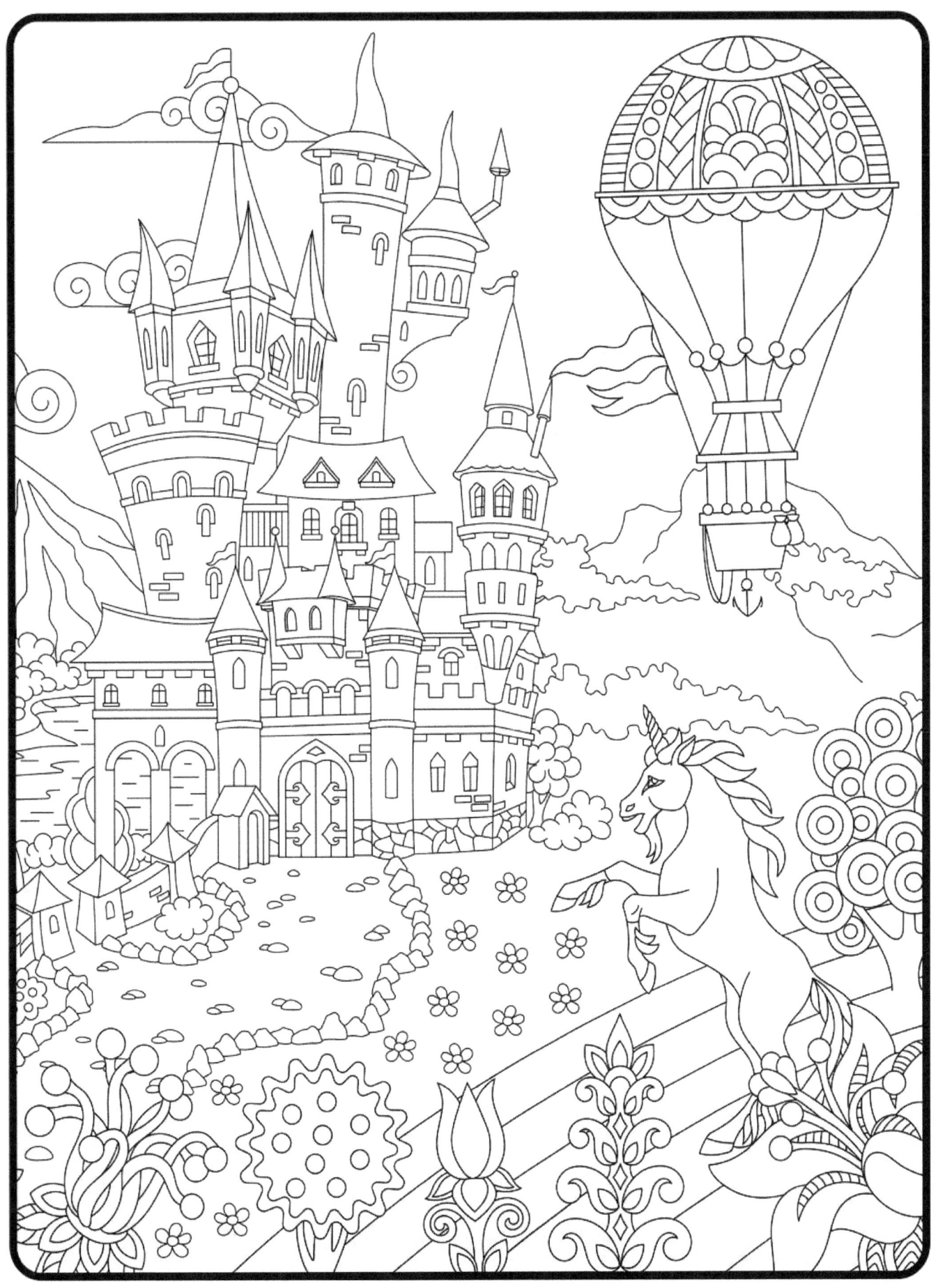

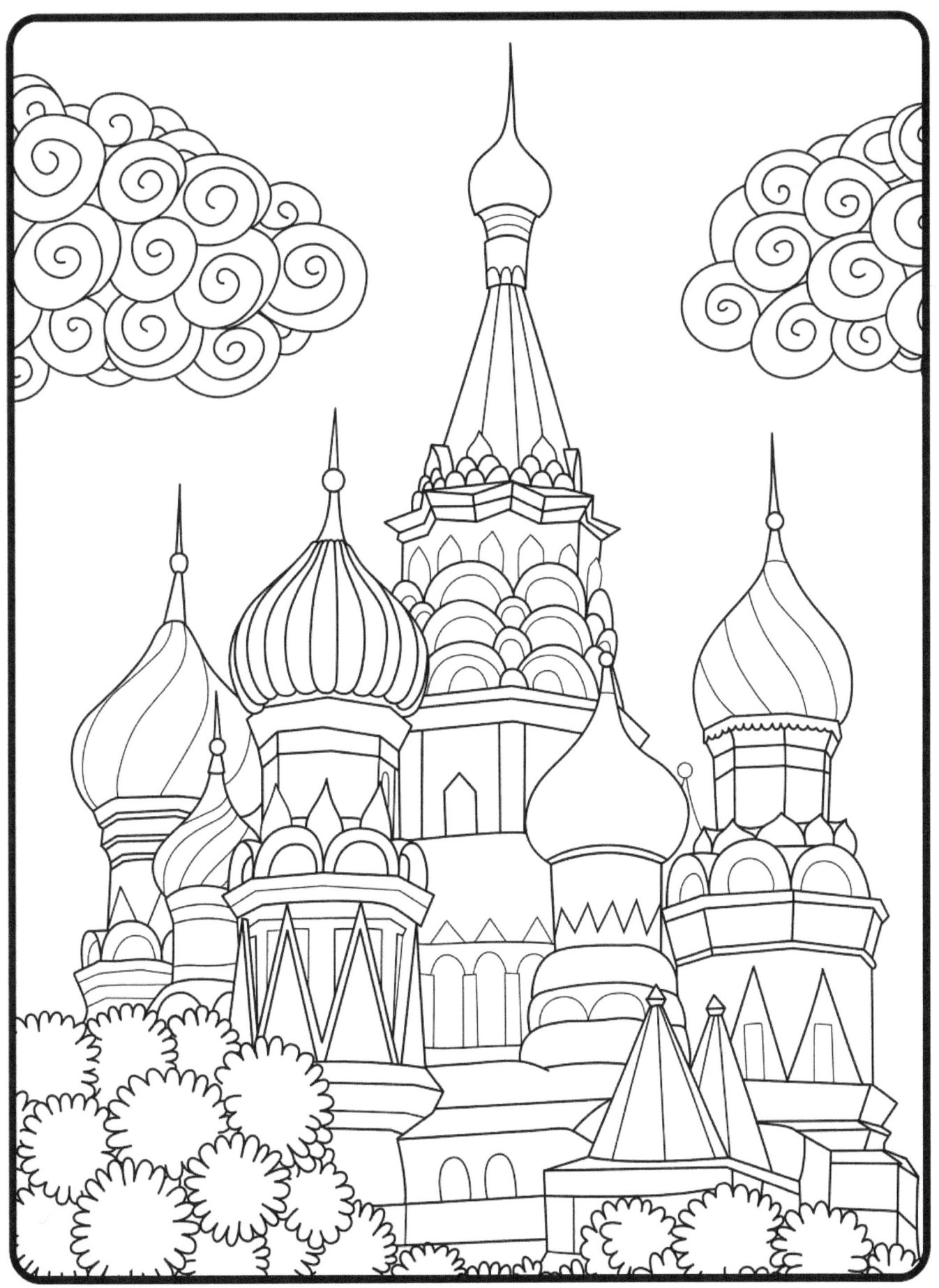

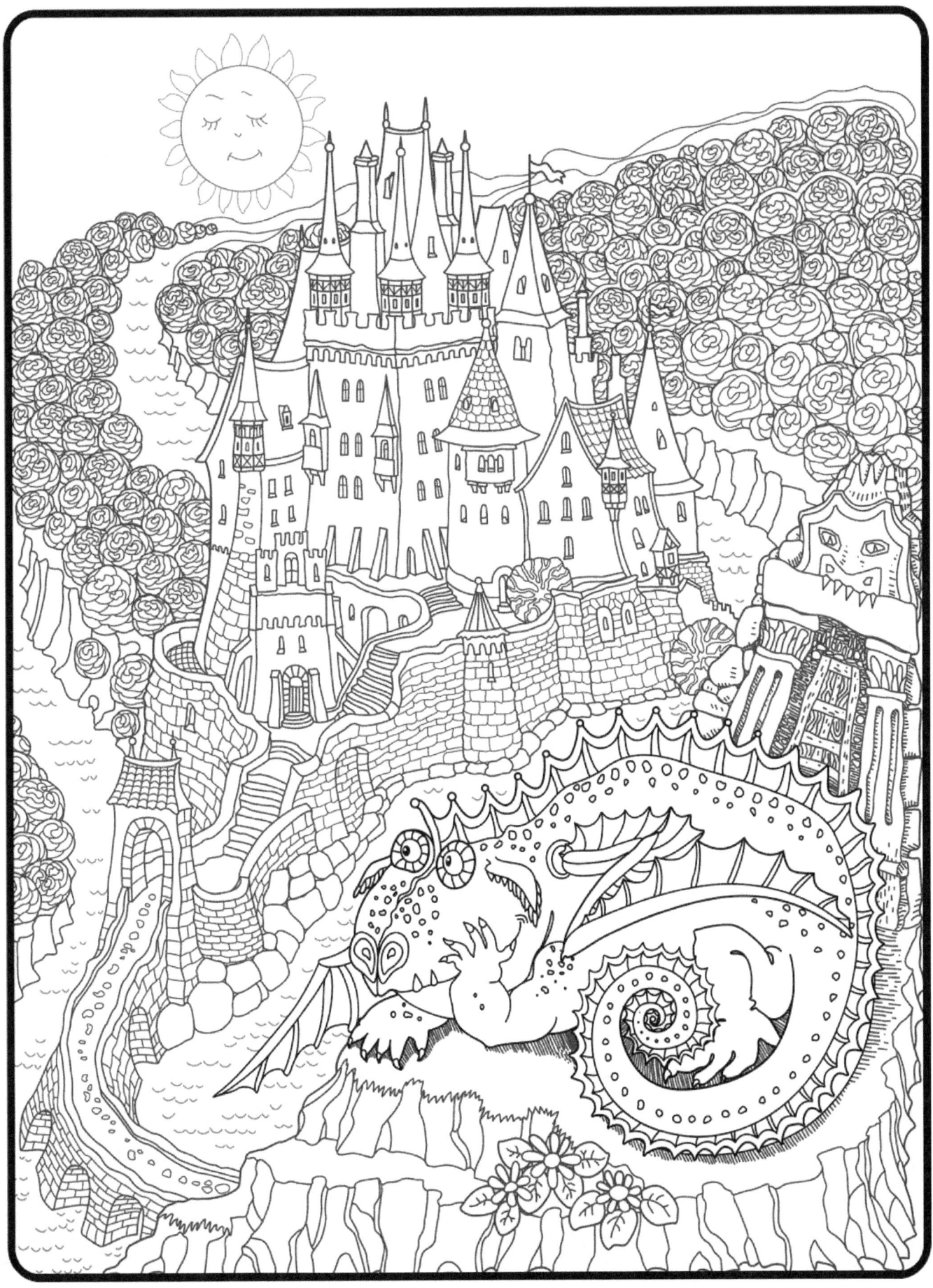

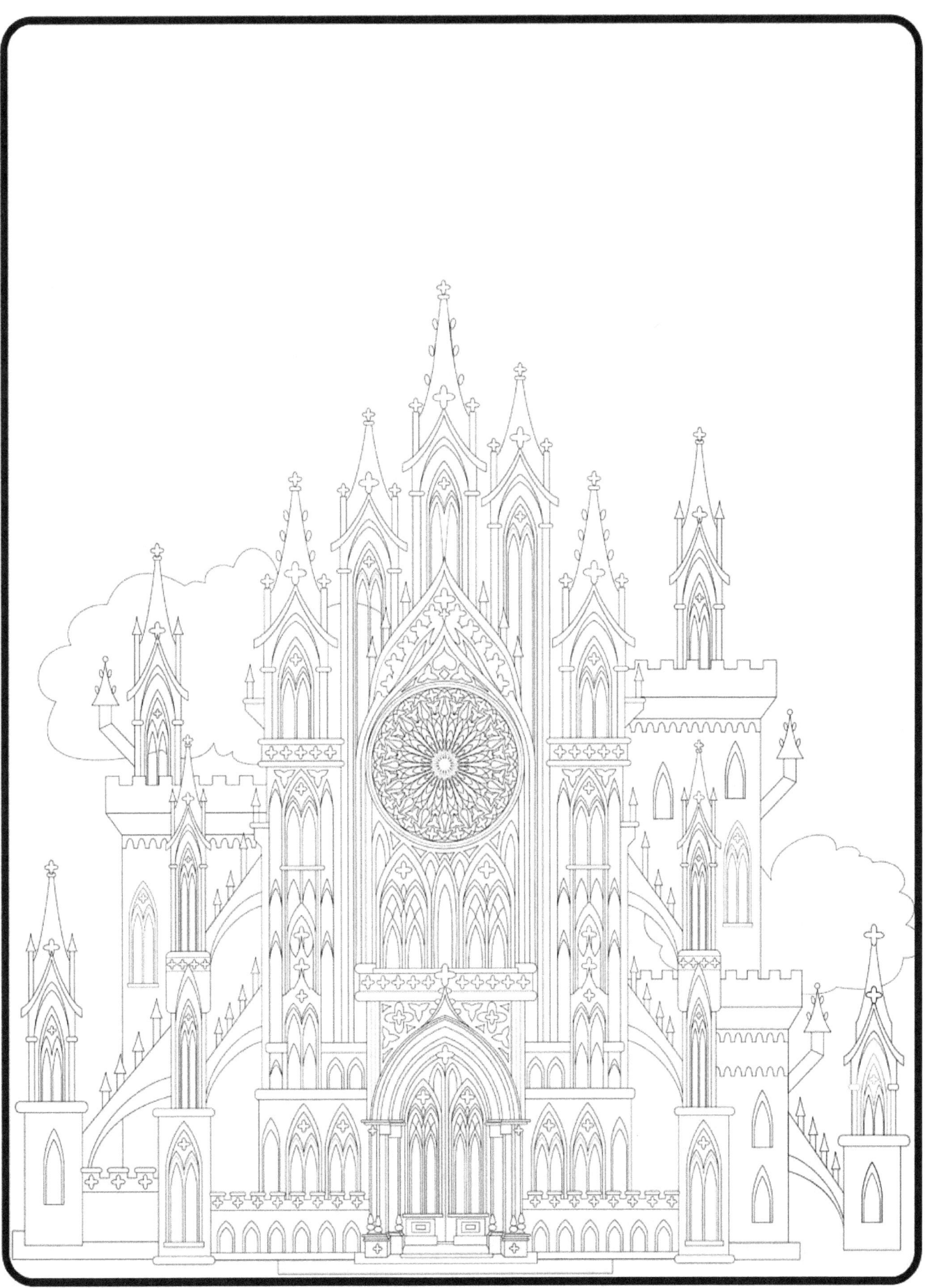

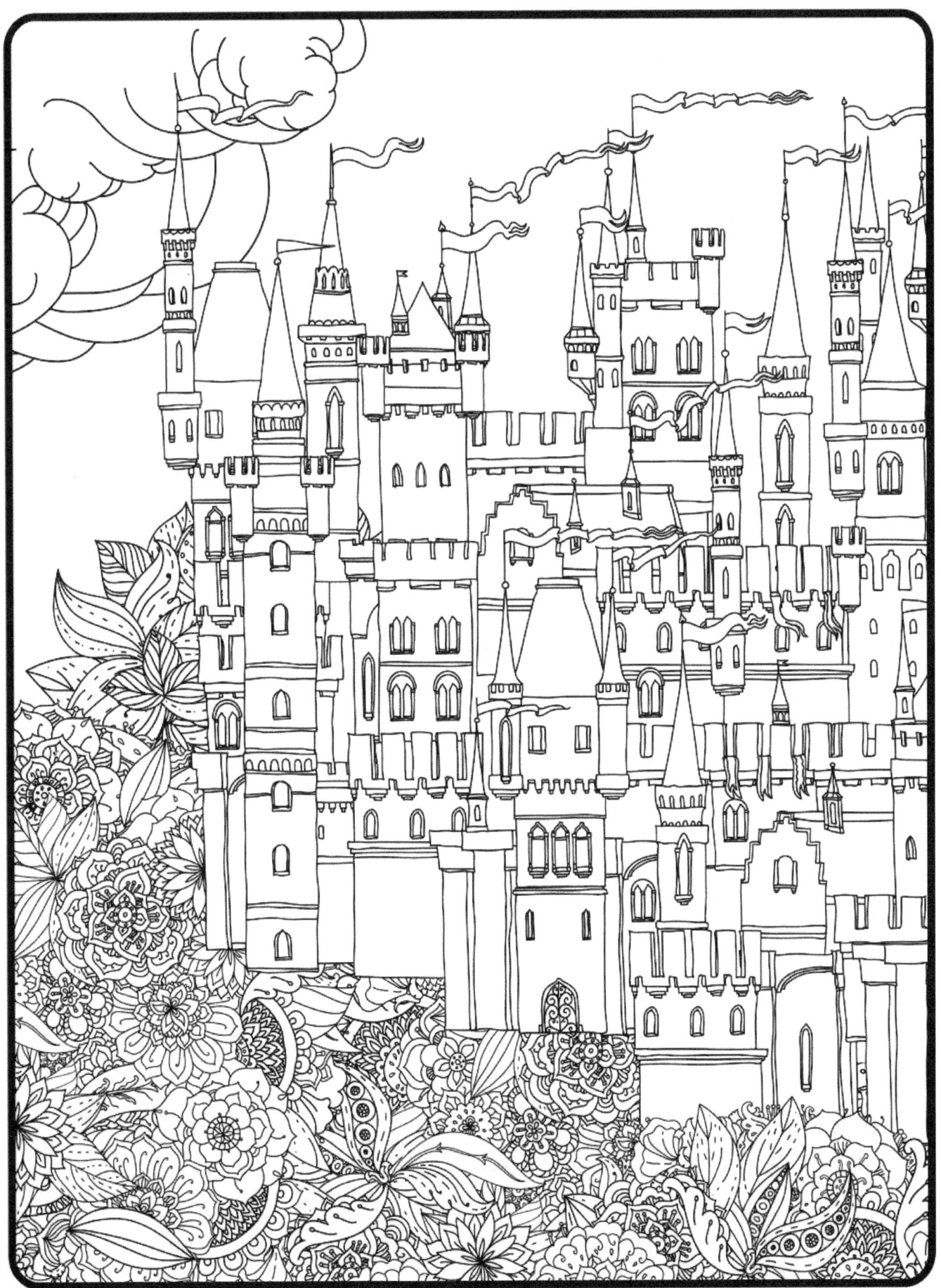

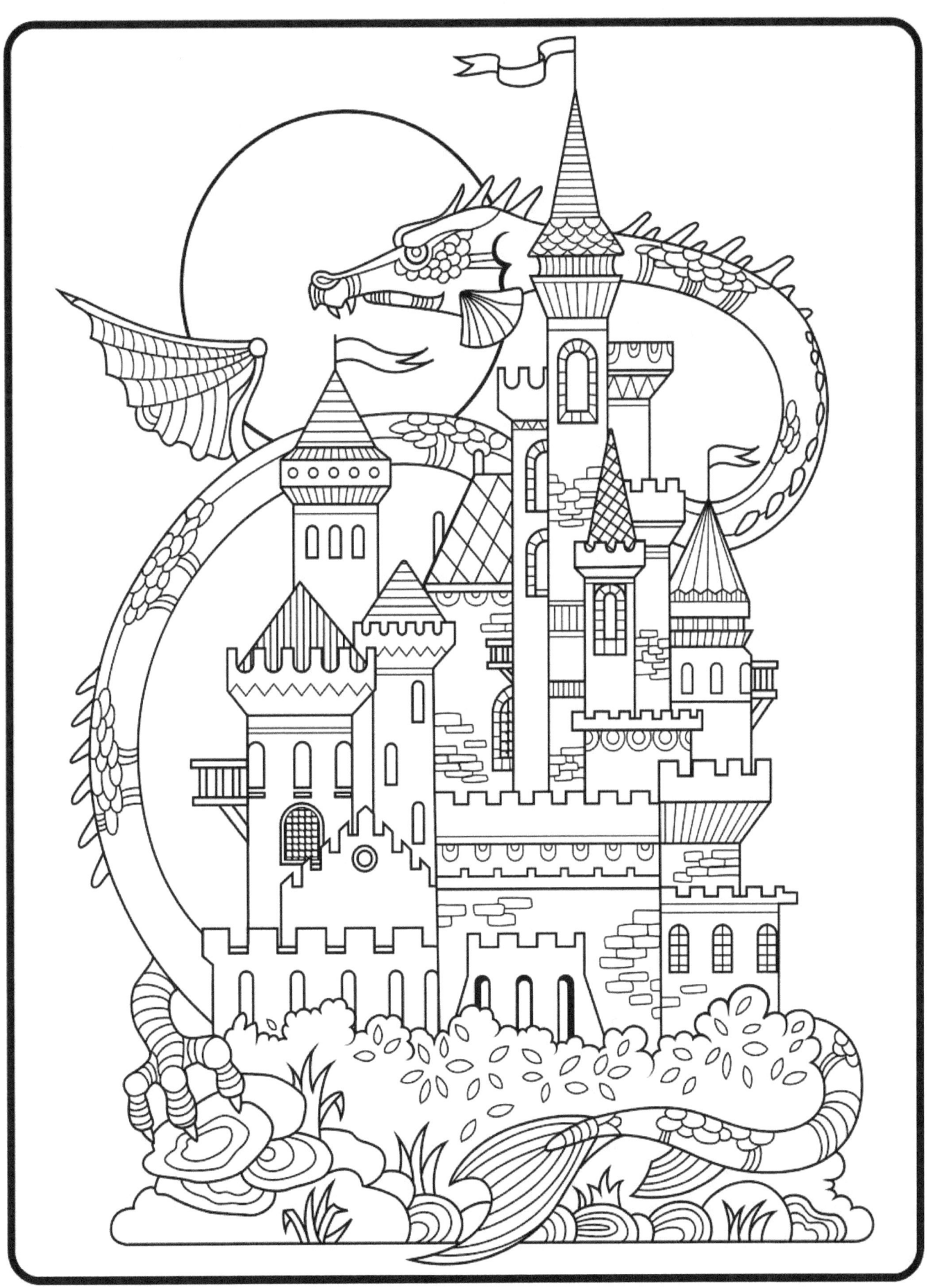

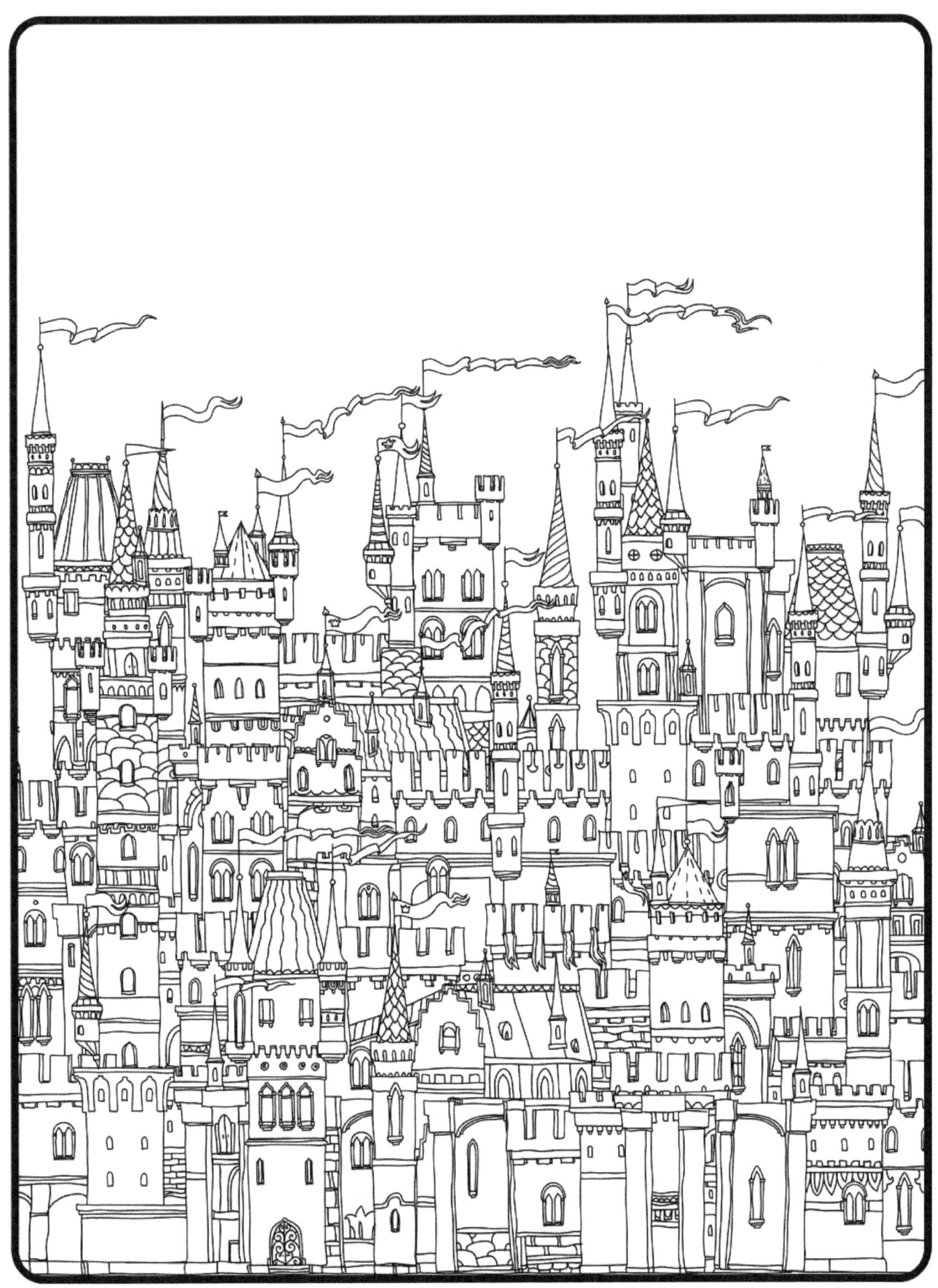

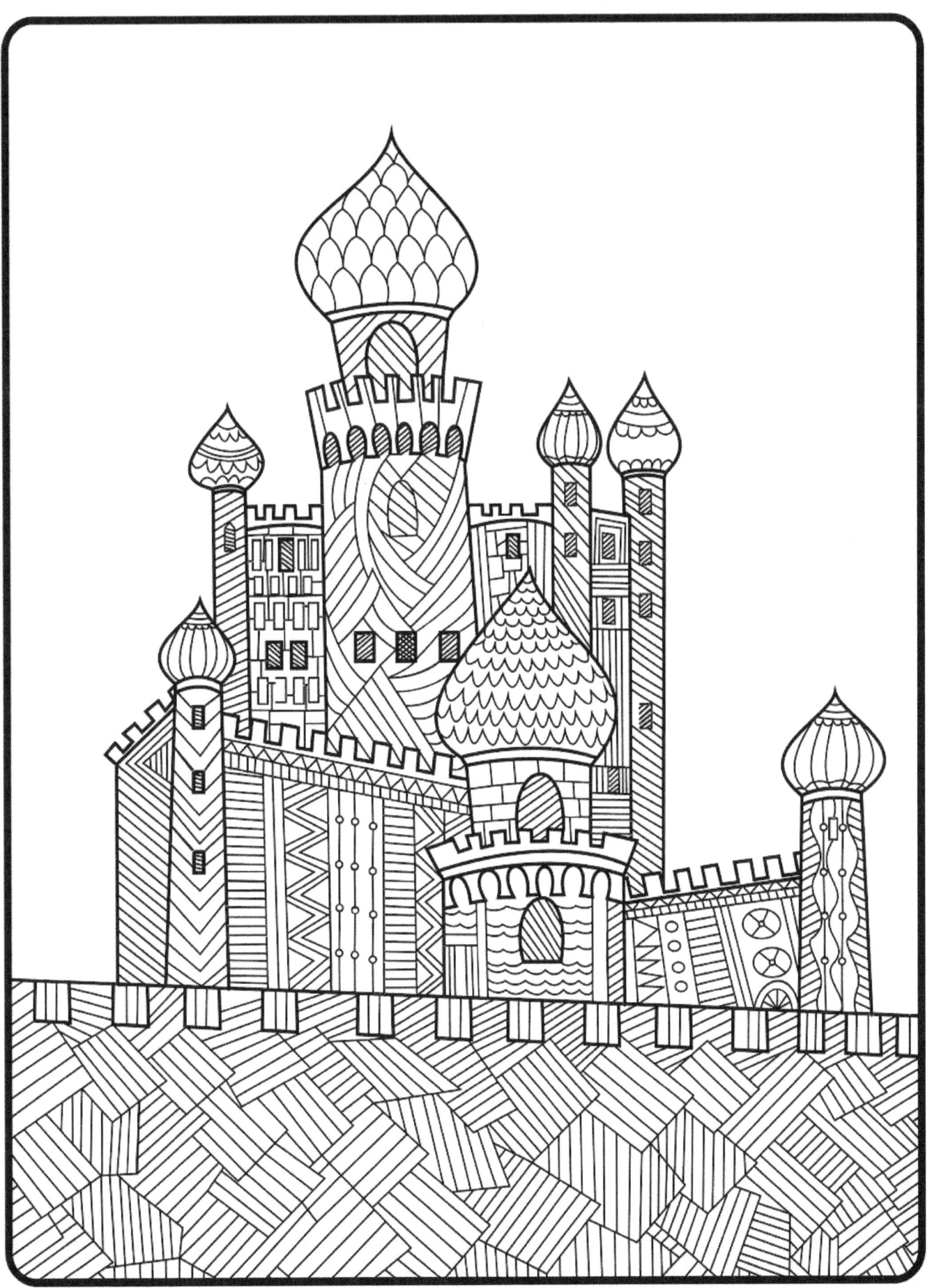

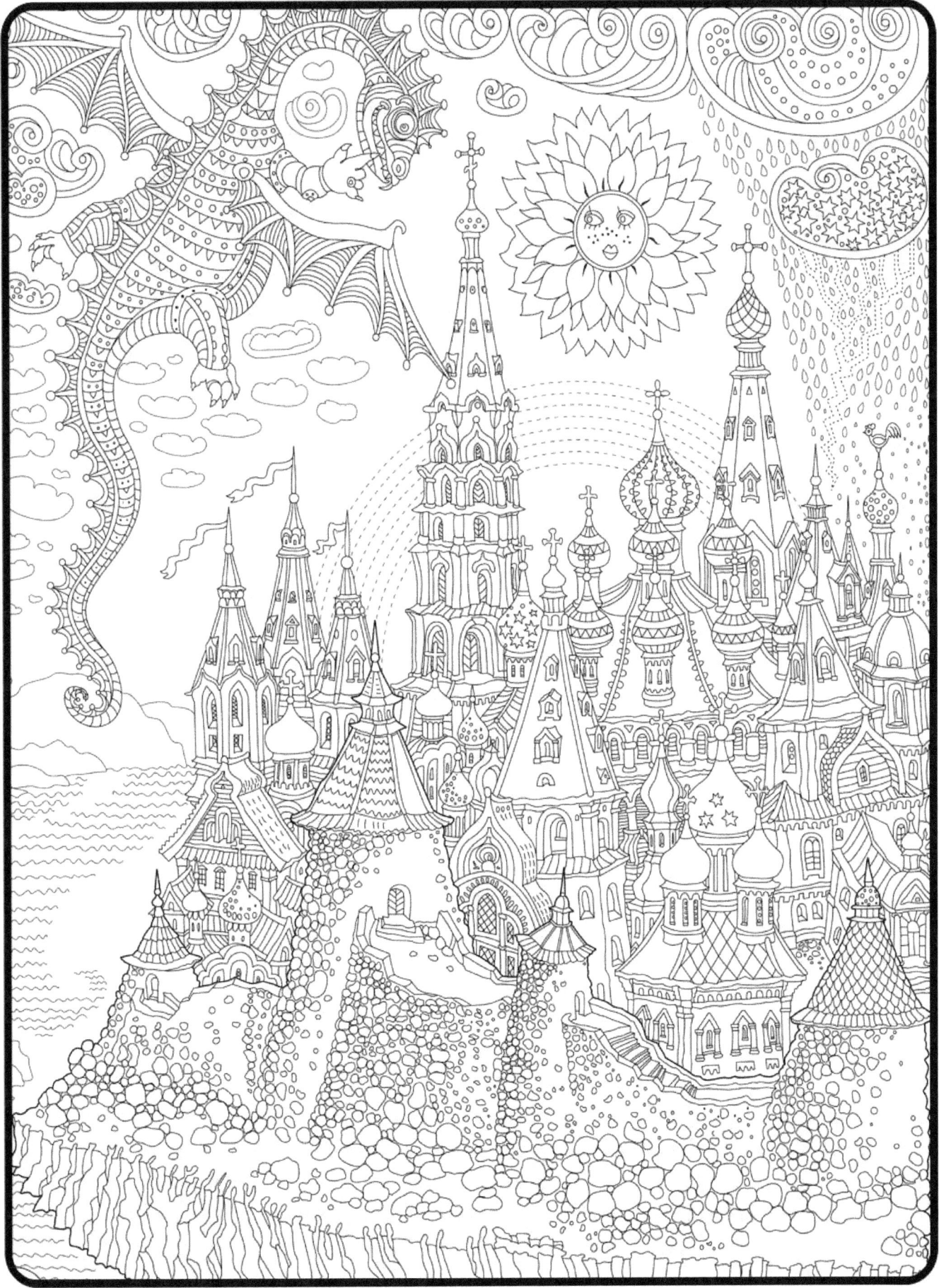

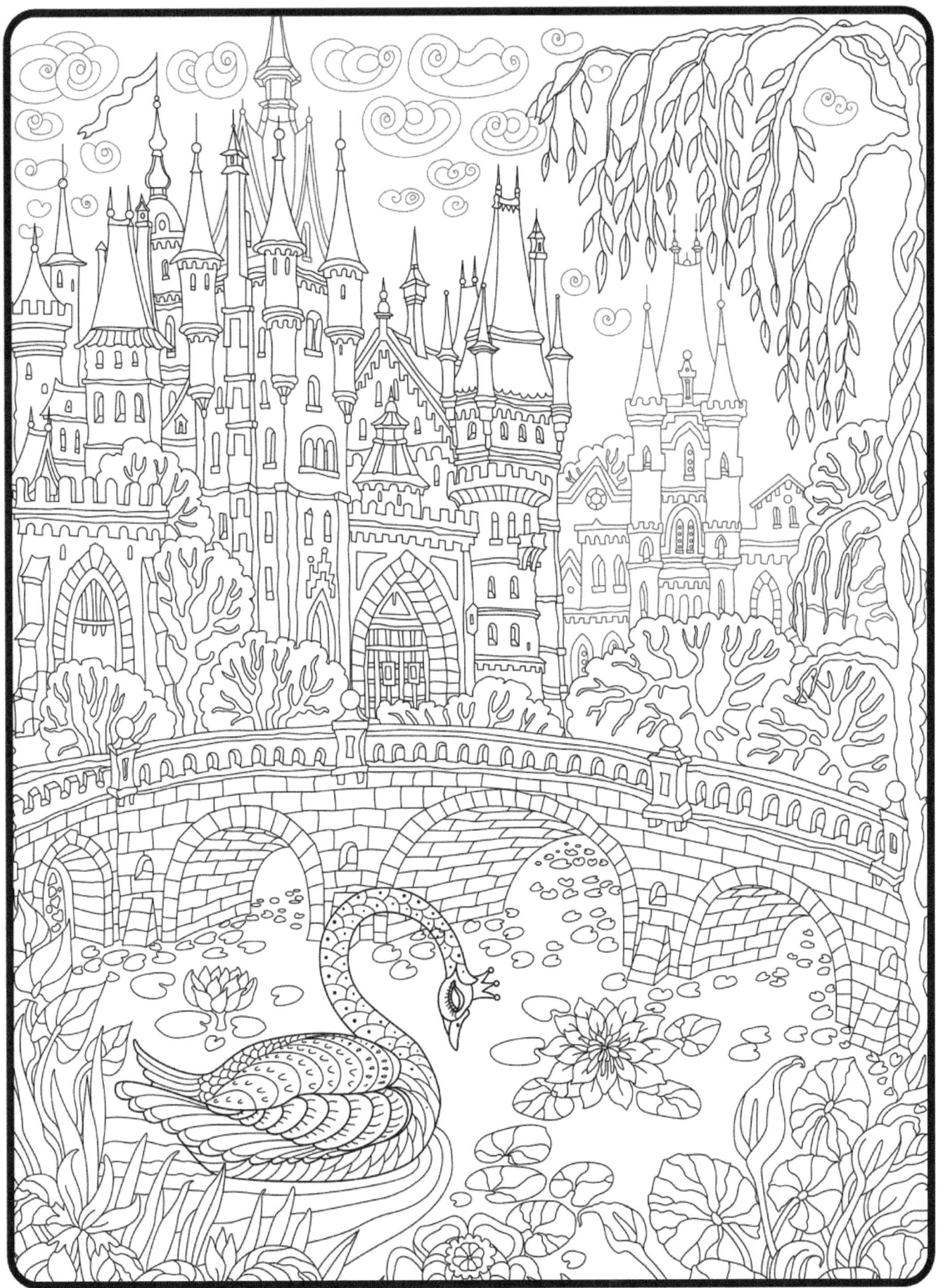

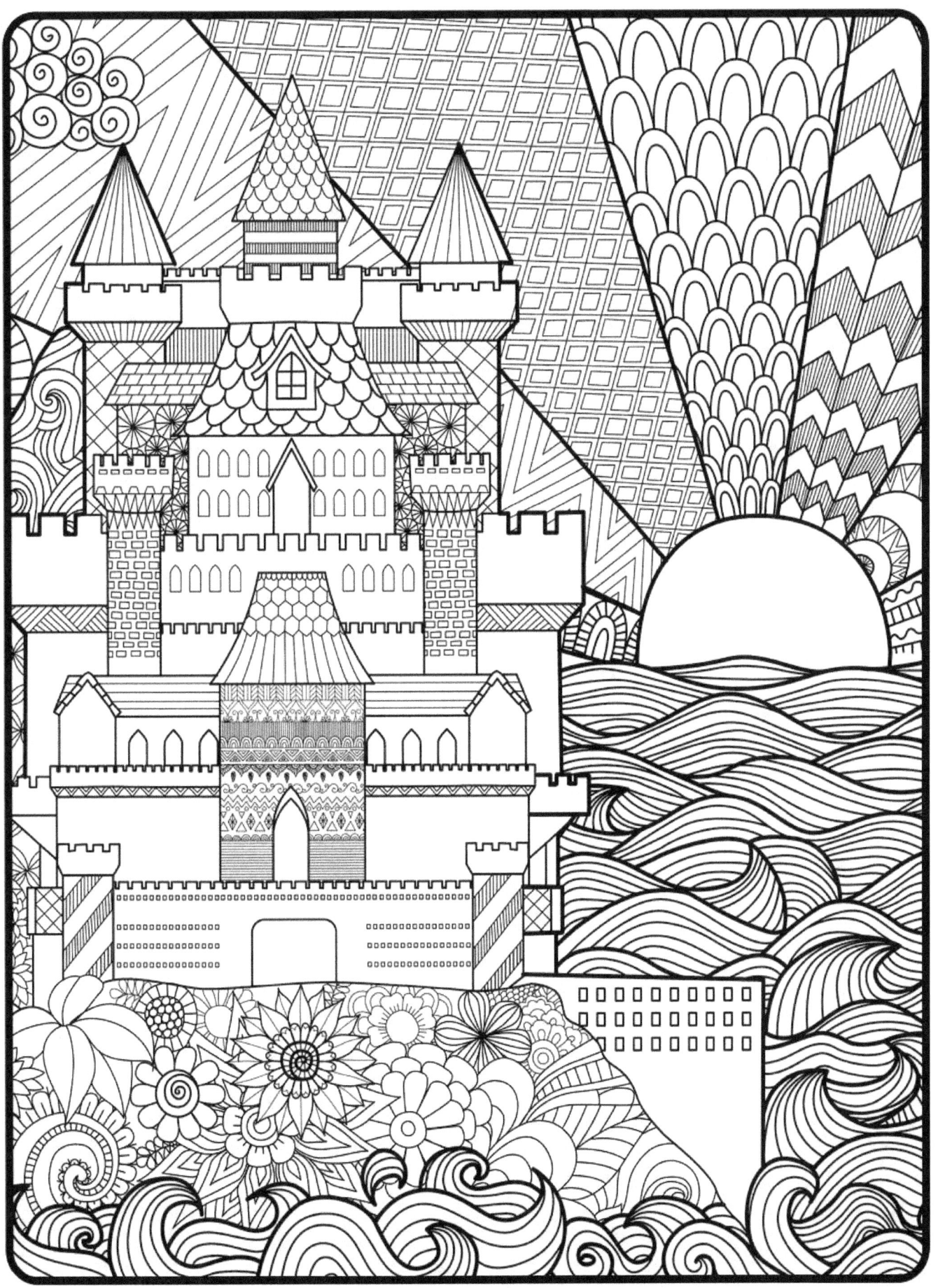

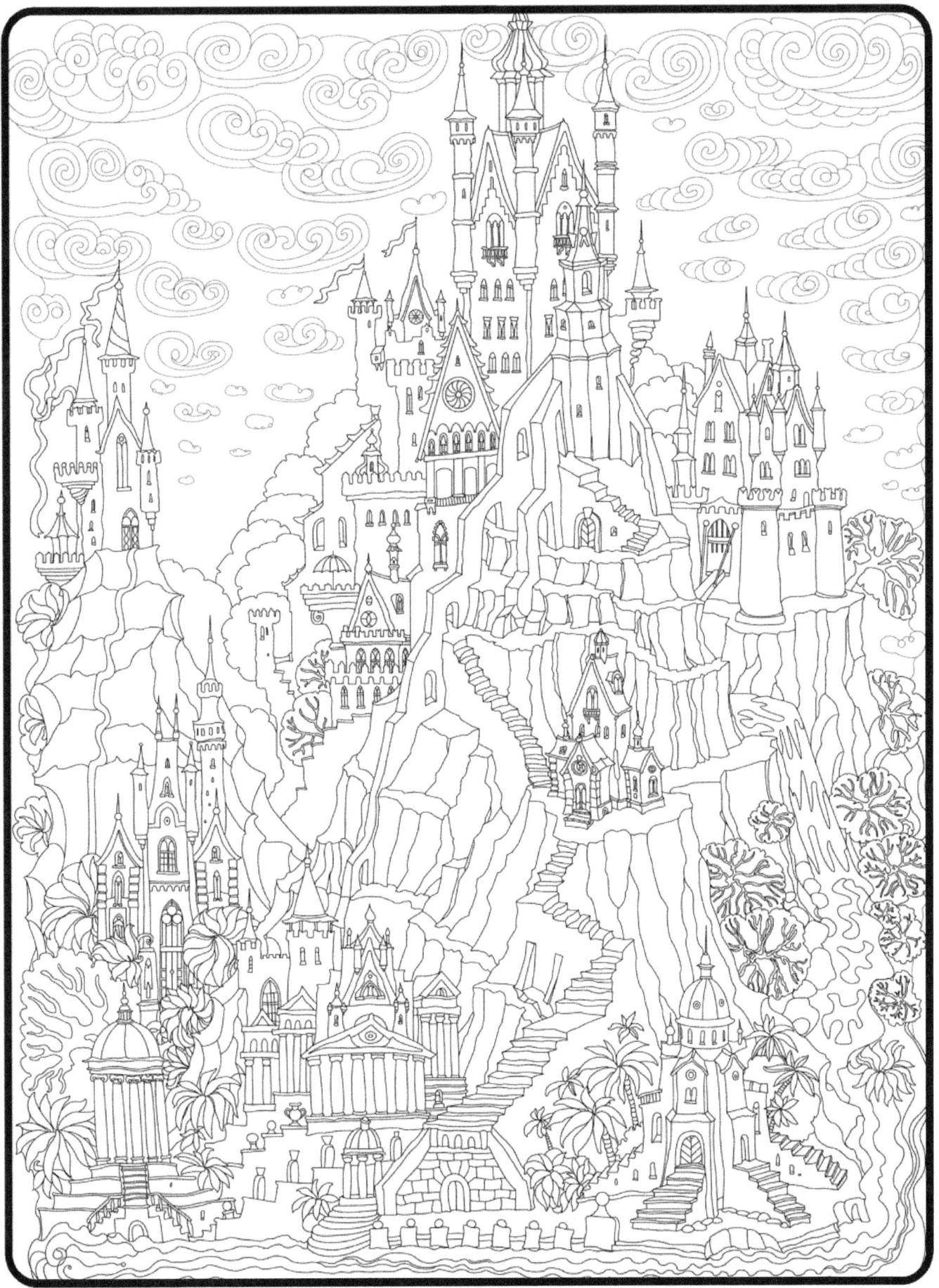

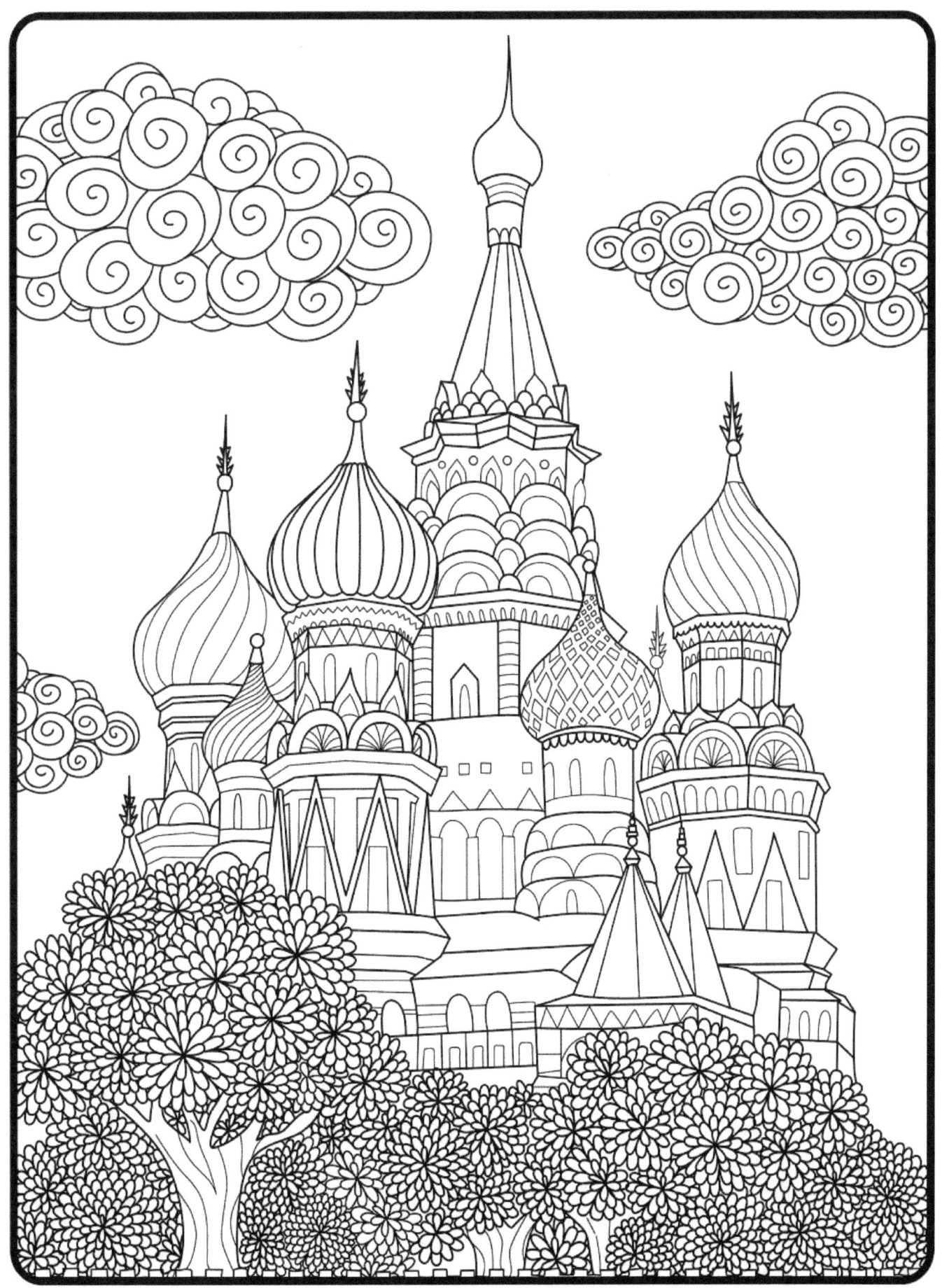

# More coloring books from Katrin Stark

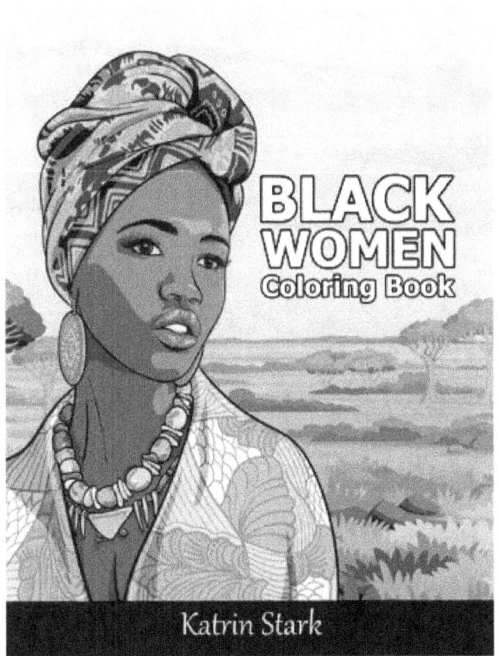

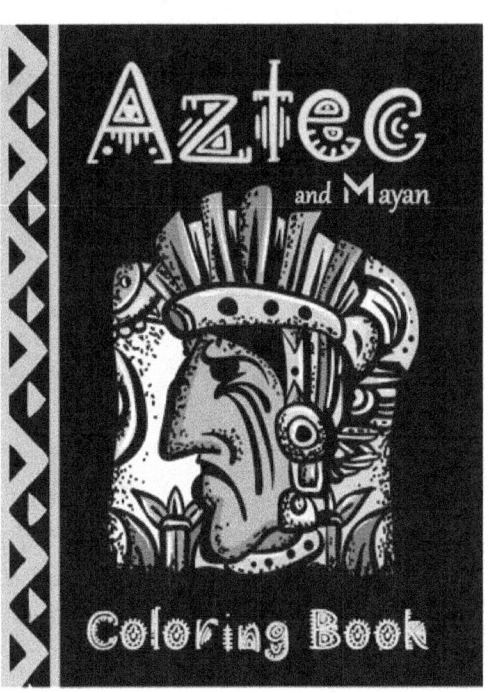

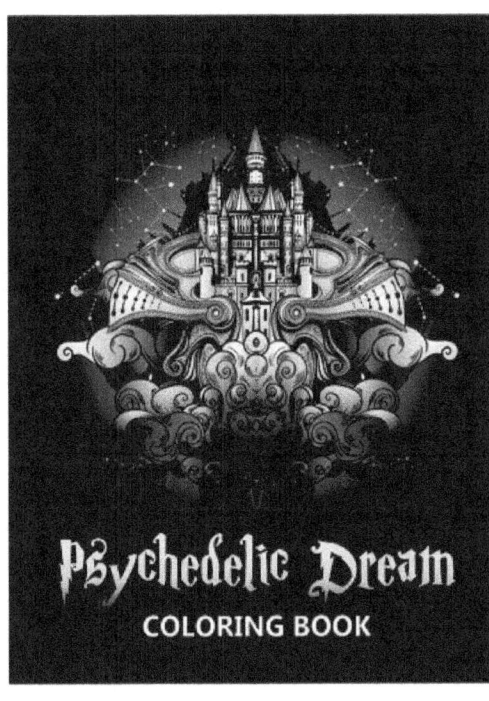

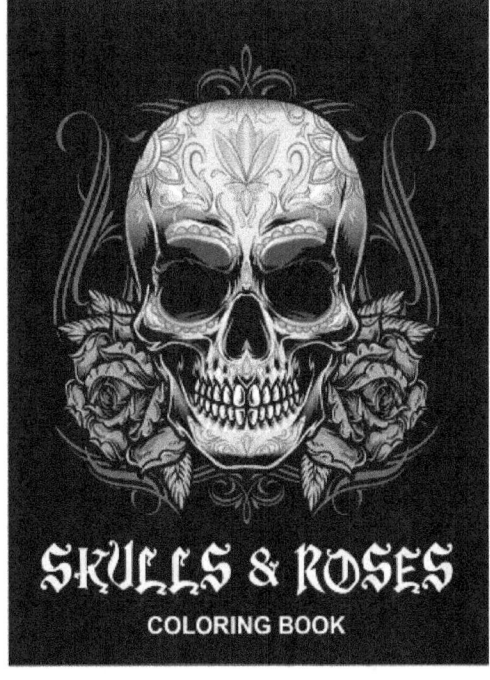

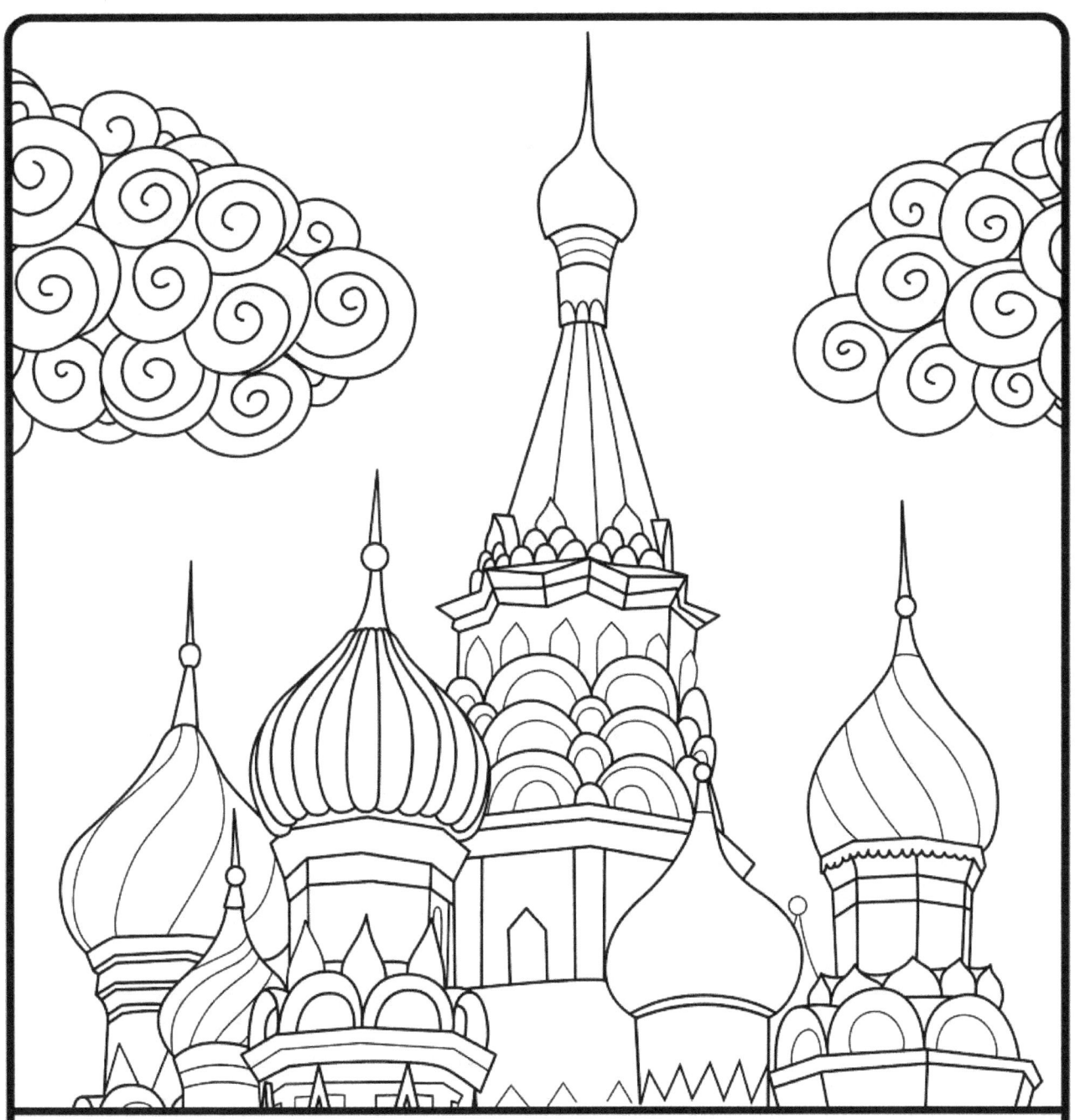

# Thank you for buying this book

If you like the book, please consider leaving a review,

it will help author to create better books in the future

www.amazon.com/Katrin-Stark
www.amazon.co.uk/Katrin-Stark